Bam Zam BOOM!

A Building Book

by EVE MERRIAM

Photo-design by WILLIAM LIGHTFOOT

SCHOLASTIC BOOK SERVICES NEW YORK · TORONTO · LONDON · AUCKLAND · SYDNEY · TOKYO

ACKNOWLEDGMENTS

Photos Courtesy: Joan A. Farber: pp. 6, 9, 13, 24; DeWys Inc: pp. 14, 16, 27; DeWys, Rosenthal: cover, pp. 21, 36; Magnum: pp. 22, 23; Magnum, Davidson: p. 29; Thomas Upshur: pp. 32-33, 40; Annan Photo Features: p. 30-31; Wide World Photos: p. 38.

TEXT COPYRIGHT © 1972 BY EVE MERRIAM. ILLUSTRATIONS COPYRIGHT © 1972 BY WILLIAM LIGHTFOOT. ALL RIGHTS RESERVED. PUBLISHED BY SCHOLASTIC BOOK SERVICES, A DIVISION OF SCHOLASTIC MAGAZINES, INCORPORATED. 1ST PRINTING...JANUARY 1972. PRINTED IN THE U.S.A.

to Roger

Bam zam!

Bam zam!

What's going on?
          Listen to the sound!

BAM

zam

bam

ZAM !

Tear the old building down to the ground.
Nothing left in it but a mean fat rat.
Knock it flat!
Bam, zam, **bam, wham!**

Bam, zam, wham away!
It's Demolition Day.

Heavy, heavy swings the wrecking ball,

Iron fist slamming, **smack** against the wall.

Crack goes the wall

  as it starts to crumble

                  Slam

                            bam

                                      zoom

DOOM!

Fall, wall...

Zonk!

Smash!

HOLD YOUR EARS FOR A

— GANGWAY —

Musty old mess

            dirty old dirt

Shovel up the rubble and cart it away.

A piece of the mantelpiece,

lead pipe, glass,

Tiles and slate and a big tin hunk —

        Clunk.

Haul it all in a barrel for junk.

Coils of wire and a window sash,

Scoop it all up in a bucket for trash.

Pry out the windows, rip up the floors.

Pick, pickaxe, pick on the painted wooden doors.

Green — yellow — pink — tan — blue —

Hanging up there, taking the air.

Call for the dumptruck and haul it all away.

        Demolition today!

When the last rubble truck is filled,

then it's time to begin to build.

And the way to begin is to

start right in

to excavate.

EX-CA-VATE?

Yes, dig a hole in the ground!

e-e-e-e-

BLAST
BLAST BOOM! BLAST
BLAST

dddrrriiiiiiiii

BLAST

B

piiiiinggg
bbbrrriiiiinggg

POWERFUL POWER!

bbbrrriiiiinggg

e-e-e-e

Ladies and gentlemen, girls and boys,
To EX-CA-VATE takes a great loud noise.

OOM!

dddrriiil|||||

///////////

FULL POWER!

Peep through the peephole in the fence and see
How deep a hole in the ground can be.
How **loud** a hole in the ground can be. BLAST!
BOOM!

Deep, deep. Deep deep down.
Dig out the gravel and sand and clay.

Deep, deep. Deeper down.
Dig out the stones that could wash away.

Deep, deeper. Dig all the way
To where there's solid ground to stay . . .

Then hold still, drill!

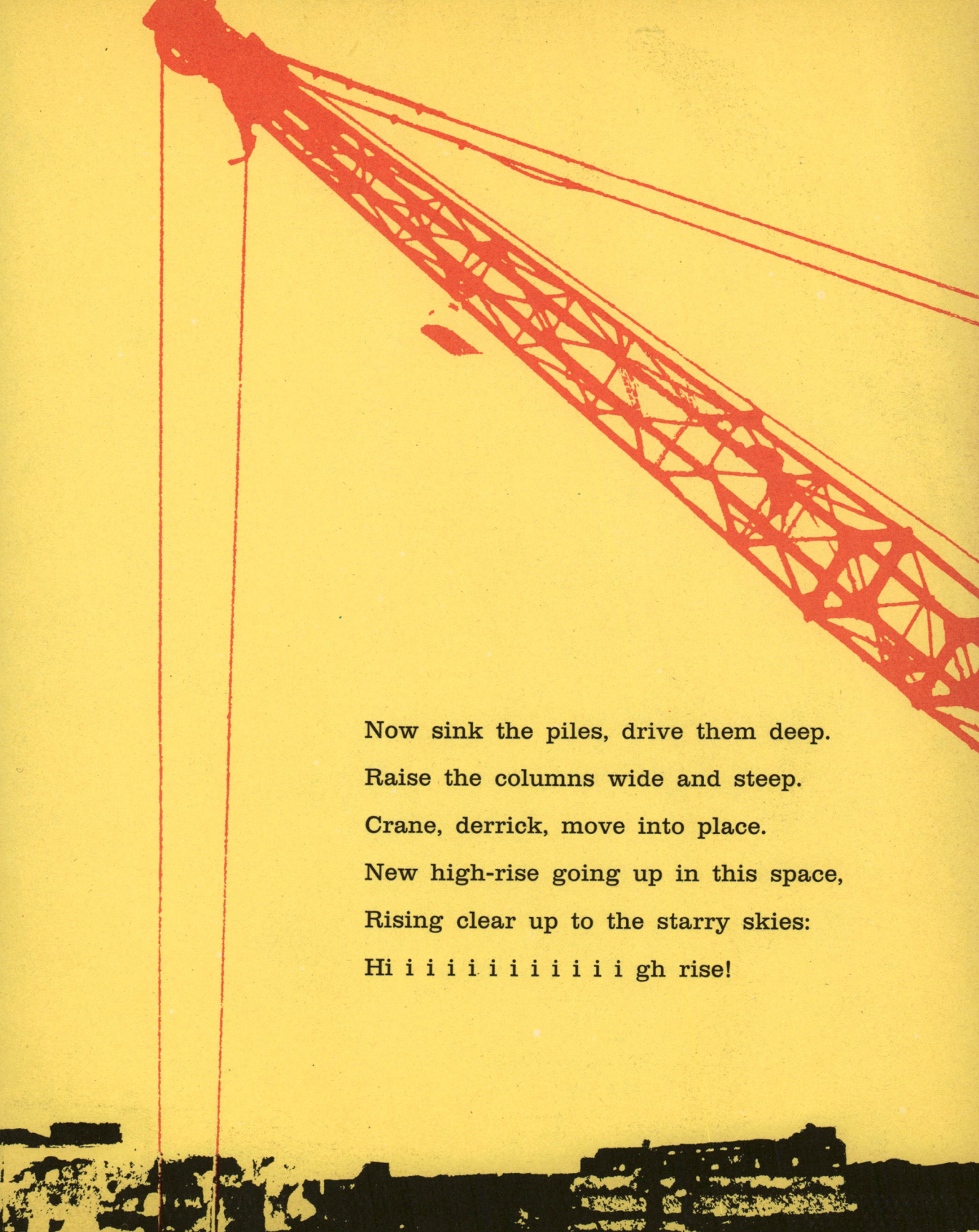

Now sink the piles, drive them deep.
Raise the columns wide and steep.
Crane, derrick, move into place.
New high-rise going up in this space,
Rising clear up to the starry skies:
Hi i i i i i i i i i i gh rise!

The crane lifts a steel beam

up from the ground.

The concrete-mixing drum whirls around.

Whirl around, drum,

whirl around and around.

Clatter and spatter

the wet concrete batter!

Pour it out later to harden and dry

To make floors to walk on up in the sky.

Hoist . . . lower . . . boom up . . . swing.
Crane reaches up. Crane stoops low.
Hoist . . . lower . . . boom up . . . swing.
Workmen show the crane how to go.

Up, up. Up up up.
The long-armed derrick lifts up a load,
Carrying cargo on the skyroad.
Giant made of metal reaches up.
Giant lifts a load and then bends low.
Slow — slow — slow — slow,

Lift, giant, lift,
Slow — slow.
Giant made of metal
go slow
but go!

Ironworker, ironworker, in a hard hat,
Balanced on a beam, graceful as a cat.
Bolt the steel columns into place,
With the sun and the wind whipping at your face.

Time out for lunch — twenty stories high!
Munch on a sandwich and a wedge of apple pie.
The edge of the wedge
Is the edge of the sky.

Hoist . . . lower . . . boom up . . . swing.
Hoist . . . lower . . . boom up . . . swing.

Up, up. Up up up —**Whoa!**

This high-rise is as high as it's going to go.

Bells, whistles, cheers,

Hip Hip Hooray!

Hoist a flag to the top floor for Topping-off Day!

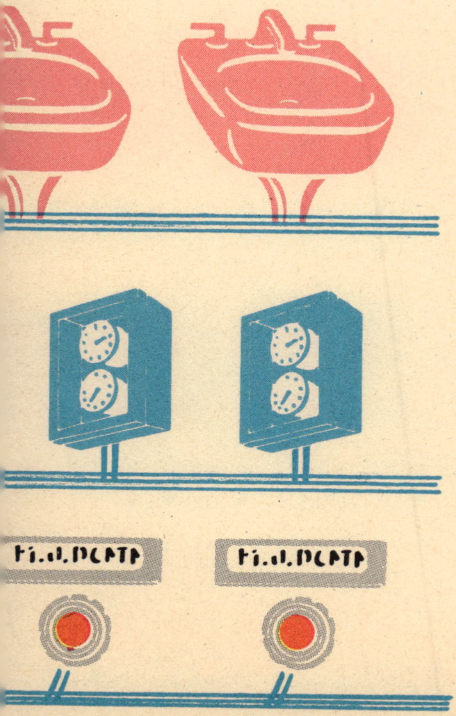

Put in the windows, Finish the floors.
Put in the sinks and stoves and doors.

Wires, light switches, flick click (click, flick!)
Telephones, doorbells and buzzers to buzz.

BUZZ-Z-Z-Z-Z-Z-Z . . .

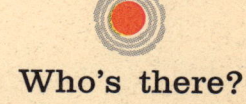

Who's there?

Moving man with the moving van.

Beds

    Chairs

        Teevees

            Toys

                Mothers and fathers —

girls and **boys!**

Welcome everybody!

Come in to stay.

At last, at last, it's Moving-In Day!

Welcome, everybody, to home in the skies
In the high high high high high hiiiiiiiiiiiigh-rise!